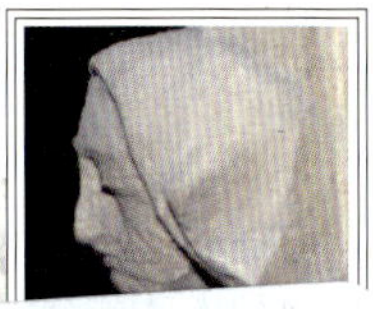

In September 1327 King Edward II, deposed King of England, was murdered while imprisoned in Berkeley Castle in southern Gloucestershire.

Though he was widely acknowledged to be a political and military failure, the former king was accorded a state funeral.

A month after his death his body, embalmed and sealed in a lead coffin, was brought to St Peter's Abbey in Gloucester (now Gloucester Cathedral).

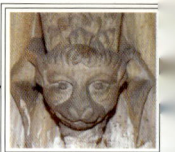

THE FUNERAL AND BURIAL

The body lay in state for two months. The bier was decorated with four lions and eight angels, all in gold; the coffin was covered with a cloth embroidered with gold leopards. The body of the king was represented by a painted wooden effigy which was dressed in robes of state. So many visitors thronged to view the body that oak barriers were needed to control the crowds.

During the splendid funeral on 20 December 1327 the king was interred just to the north of the altar. The grave was initially marked by a simple Purbeck 'marble' slab, on which perhaps was placed the effigy that had been carried in the funeral procession.

Soon a magnificent tomb was raised over the burial, incorporating the initial slab in its base plinth. The tomb was completed in less than ten years. We know this because after 1337 the old Romanesque choir was converted to a soaring Gothic structure which was specially designed with a flying arch to accommodate the king's tomb.

Designed by a London master mason, probably employed by the royal family, the tomb is built of three different types of stone: oolitic limestone (from near Gloucester), Purbeck 'marble' (a hard grey-green limestone from Dorset) and alabaster for the effigy (from the Nottingham area).

Opposite: The finished tomb.

The first tomb was a Purbeck marble funerary slab on a limestone base. The initial phase in the construction of the final tomb involved the building of a kerb of oolitic limestone around the original stone.

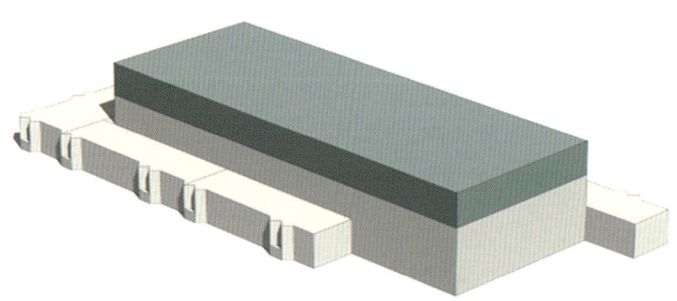

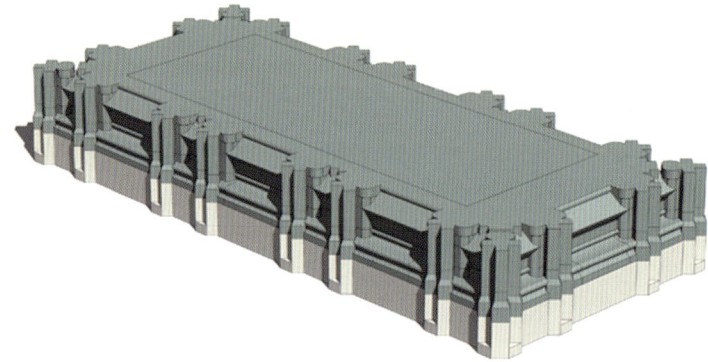

Above the limestone kerb, a carved plinth of Purbeck marble was added. The plinth was built up to the level of the primary funerary slab.

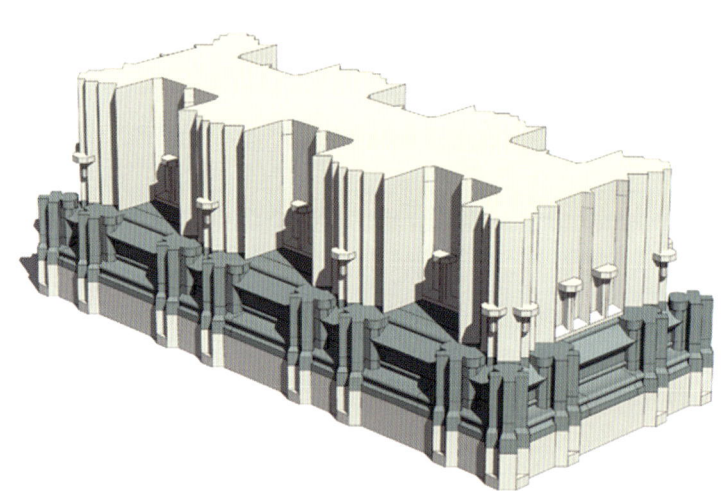

Large blocks of limestone form the core of the tomb, built on top of the primary funerary slab.

In front of the limestone, rising from the Purbeck marble base plinth, is a series of angled shafts which were jointed into the limestone with deep V-shaped sockets.

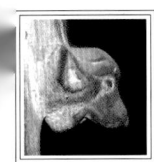
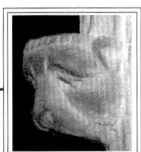

The capital, now rather damaged, of one of the columns carved onto the side faces of the angled Purbeck marble shafts.

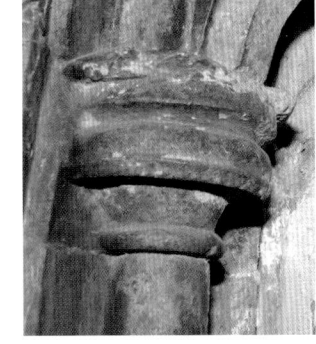

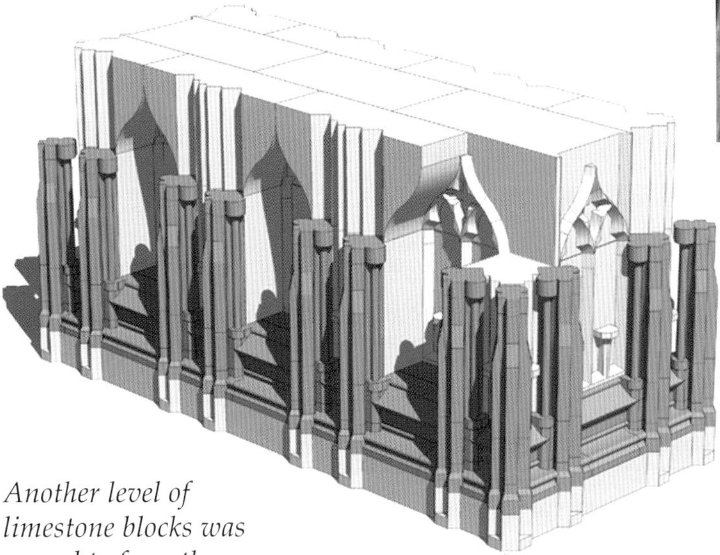

Another level of limestone blocks was carved to form the arched tops and blind tracery back panels of the niches.

This upper level of limestone blocks was then faced with large Purbeck marble panels, two on each side and a single panel on each end.

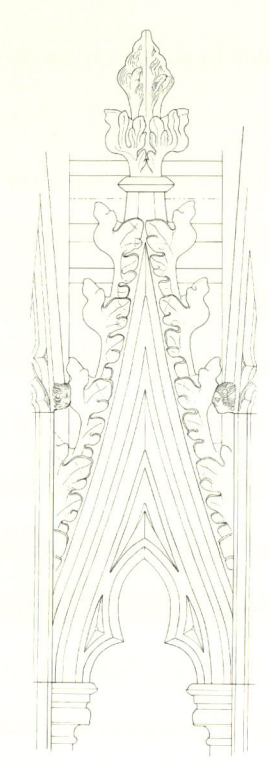

Above and left: Reconstructions of the ogee arch heads carved onto the Purbeck marble facing panels. The pairs of holes above the arches of the larger niches held metal shields showing the arms of the noble relatives represented by the statues in the niches below.

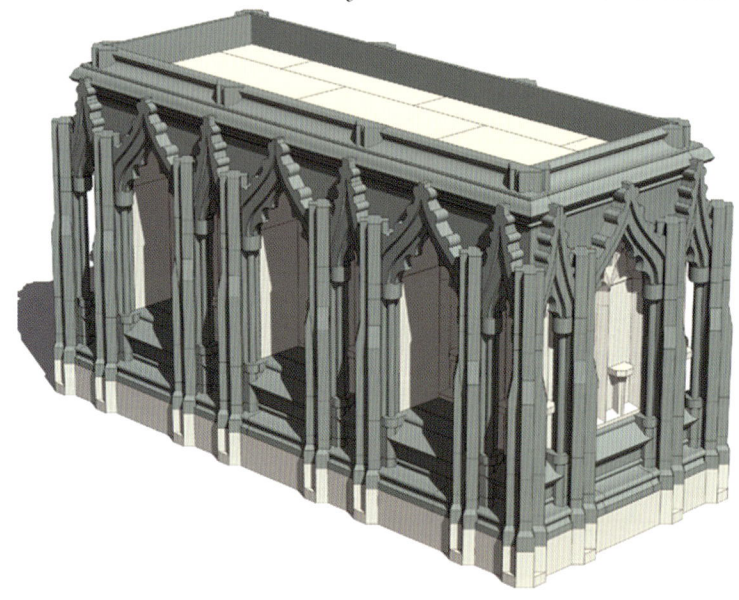

The facing panels carry much of the detailed carving for the upper part of the chest tomb, including ogee arches, the upper portions of the angled shafts and the mouldings that surround the top.

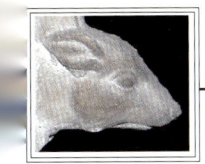

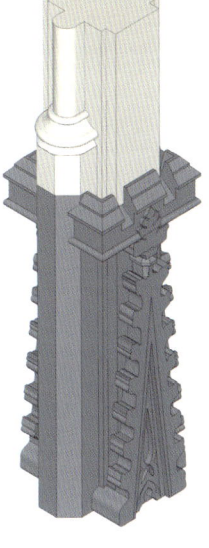

Details of the plant forms carved onto the sides of the crenellated collars

The angled shafts around the chest tomb were finished with a set of intricately carved and crenellated collars, designed as support seatings for the flying buttresses of the canopy level.

The chest tomb was completed by adding limestone slabs to the top, inside the Purbeck edge moulding. These slabs were then stained to match the Purbeck marble.

Right: Statues also once stood on the plinths in the narrower niches. The twelve figures may have been the apostles.

Right: The funerary weeper statue of a king from the tomb of Edward II's son, John of Eltham, in Westminster Abbey.

The backs of the sixteen larger niches were originally painted and still contain plinths and fixing points for statues of noble relatives of the king. These funerary statues are sometimes called weepers.

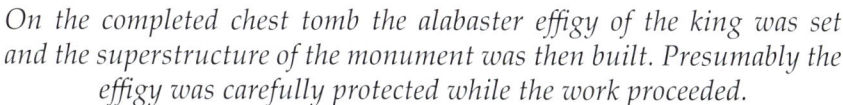

On the completed chest tomb the alabaster effigy of the king was set and the superstructure of the monument was then built. Presumably the effigy was carefully protected while the work proceeded.

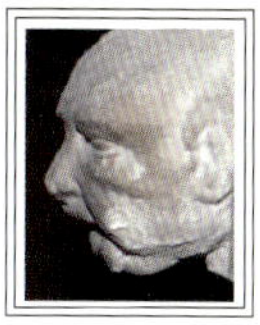

The alabaster effigy represents the earliest use of this material for the tomb of an English monarch. Jewels were originally set into the crown, and the effigy was probably also painted. The face of the king is not intended to be a realistic portrait. Instead the sculptor, almost certainly a court mason, has 'transferred into stone the illuminators' conventional representation of God'. The cushions under the King's head are supported by angels, while a placid lion lies at his feet. The effigy is liberally covered with mostly 18th-century graffiti: the likely culprits were Kings School boys of that time.

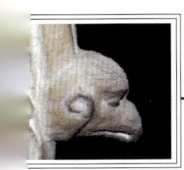

Poppy-head finial.

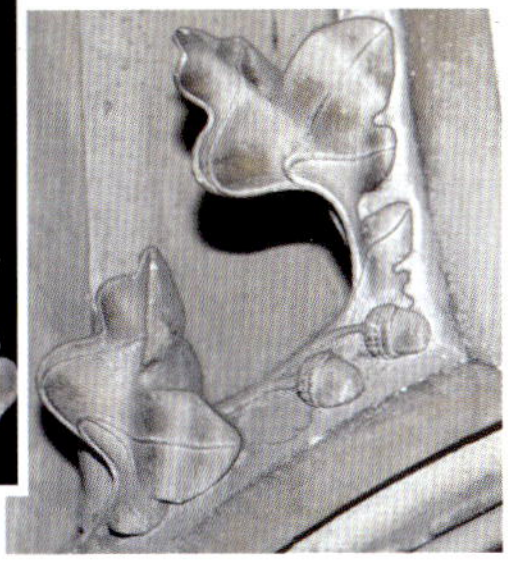

The leaf and acorn motif used on the canopy arches above the effigy.

☐ Limestone
☐ Alabaster
▨ Purbeck

The plan and section of the monument show how the different materials were used.

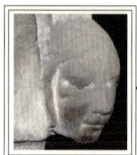
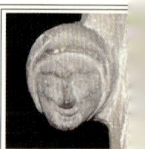

The decorated bracket between one of the canopy shafts and its supporting flying buttress.

The canopy is supported on eight limestone shafts with attached columns: these are seated partly on the limestone chest tomb and partly on the Purbeck marble facing. The eight shafts are in turn supported by 20 flying buttresses seated in the Purbeck marble collars on the top of angled shafts.

 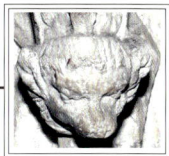

Above the effigy the canopy consists of three linked vaults each of square plan.

Left: One of the central bosses from the canopy vault above the effigy.

Right: The 'Halls of Heaven' looking from the west

Below: On the upper side of the canopy vault, lies a 'hall' also with three canopies supported on clusters of slender columns. The stone floor of this upper hall contains pairs of dowel holes which may have supported statues. Perhaps these were angels and the upper tier was intended to represent the heavenly region, the 'Halls of Heaven', at which the king appears to be gazing.

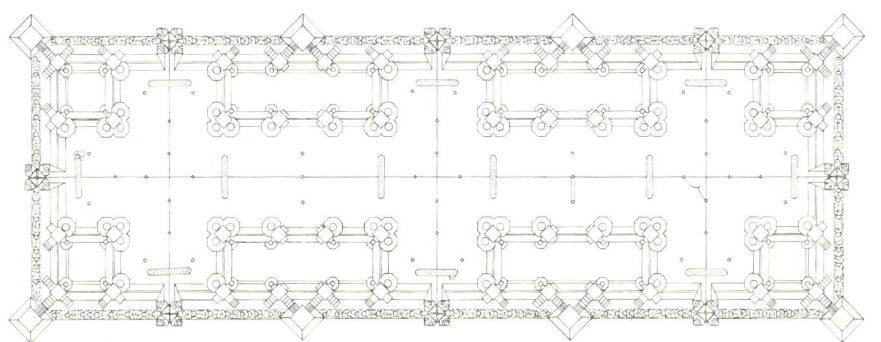

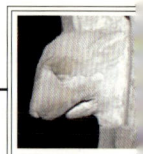

From the floor level of the upper hall the monument rises in three separate towers, surmounted by openwork spires. Each tower has four 'corner turrets' each with its own central openwork spirelet. The whole of the superstructure is further enhanced with finials, ogee-arched gables, crockets, poppy heads, and beast and human head label-stops.

Right: Each corner turret is almost entirely carved from one piece of stone. To make one of these turrets would take 500 hours: twelve would thus take 3 years of a mason's time: and this is only one part of the monument.

Left: Drawing of the tomb from the west

Right: A canopy vault from the Halls of Heaven

Below: plan view looking up into the three separate high-level canopy vaults over the Halls of Heaven. Above these rise three spires.

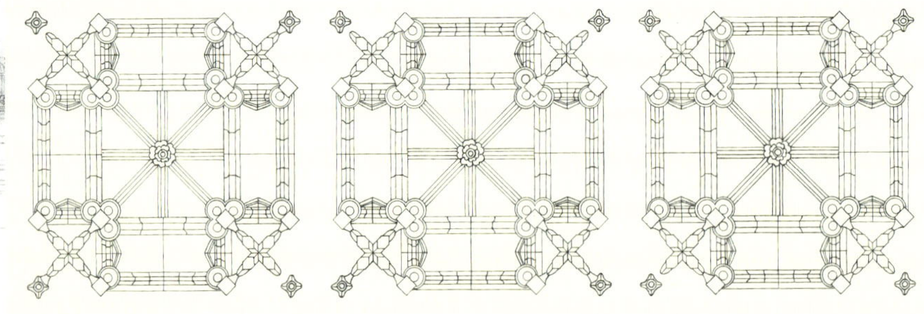

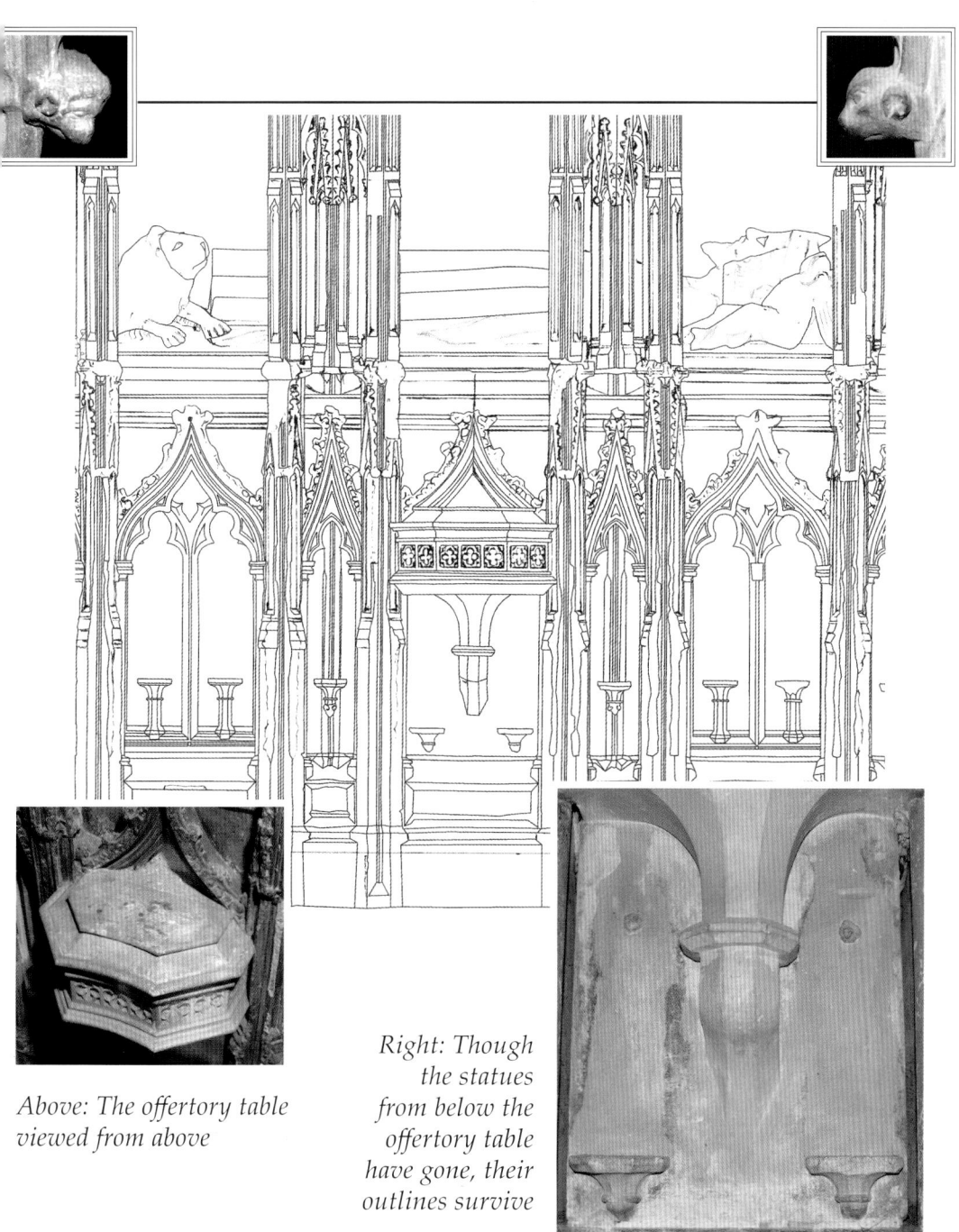

Above: The offertory table viewed from above

Right: Though the statues from below the offertory table have gone, their outlines survive

On the north side of the monument is a carved offertory table with quatrefoil decoration. This has been added to the tomb by inserting a massive block of limestone 80 cm deep into the central main niche. It may have been made to carry the golden ship given by Edward III c. 1350. The statues displaced by this process were repositioned below the table.

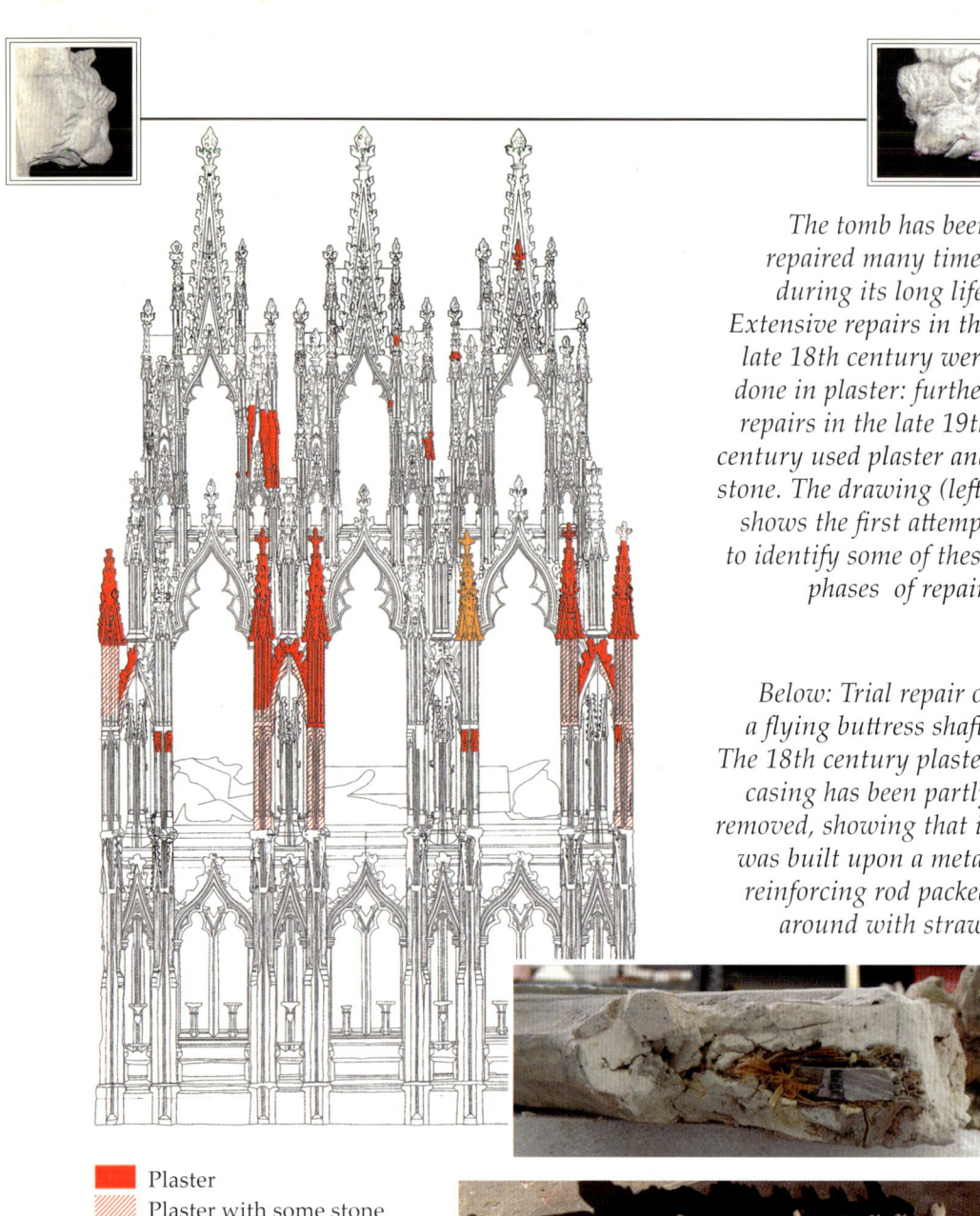

The tomb has been repaired many times during its long life. Extensive repairs in the late 18th century were done in plaster: further repairs in the late 19th century used plaster and stone. The drawing (left) shows the first attempt to identify some of these phases of repair.

Below: Trial repair of a flying buttress shaft. The 18th century plaster casing has been partly removed, showing that it was built upon a metal reinforcing rod packed around with straw.

■ Plaster
▨ Plaster with some stone
■ 19th/20th century stone

Right: In 1875 many details were replaced with good quality carving, some of which has come loose.

Published by Past Historic, Kings Stanley, Stonehouse, Gloucestershire 2007   ISBN 978 0 9557093 0 2
Text © Carolyn Heighway and Richard Bryant 2007

All photographs and drawings © Gemma Bryant and Richard Bryant 2007, except for p. 2 detail of Edward II from the Great East Window (www.skycell.net); pp. 3, 10 and front cover - tomb and effigy (Angelo Hornak/ Gloucester Cathedral 2006); p. 16 trial repair (Hailes and Howe). The funerary weeper (p. 8) Gemma Bryant, by courtesy of the Dean and Chapter of Westminster. Back cover illustration Gemma Bryant and Thomas Fowlie.

All rights reserved. No part of this publication may be reproduced by any means without the permission of Past Historic and the copyright holders.   Printed in Great Britain